HELP! MY CHILD IS PESCATARIAN

HEALTHY RECIPES FOR THE ENTIRE FAMILY

AUNTEA MUHAMMAD & AFUW MUHAMMAD JR

A SOLUTION FOR BUSY MOMS

HI :)

Afuw at 6 years old, with me, when we started this journey.

Afuw at 13 years old, with me!

My name is Auntea (ahn-tay-yah). I am a full-time mom to a rapidly growing 13-year-old pescatarian, a full-time employee at a major Fortune 500 company, and a serial entrepreneur running an LLC and a nonprofit, just to name a few. Needless to say, I am a pretty busy mom every day.

I imagine it is difficult for all moms to create an interesting meal palate for their children, but it certainly adds pressure when your child is a pescatarian (and you are not), a naturally picky-eater, and fairly opinionated, thanks to his gene pool. On top of all of that, add two full virtual schedules during a pandemic, and that's where the journey to creating this book began.

Like most moms, I desire my son to eat healthy, enjoy his meals, and learn to enjoy cooking based on his childhood traditions. At times, I felt like I was failing him in this area so I decided to do something about it, as well as help other moms that are in the same boat as me.

A SOLUTION FOR BUSY MOMS

INTRODUCTION

I decided to create this recipe book for moms raising pescatarian children because I know the struggle. After limiting eating-out due to the pandemic in 2020, and after surviving several occasions of cross-contamination at restaurants, I was determined to find and create more meals to satisfy my then-8-year-old's fairly small palate. There is only so much salmon one can take! Whenever I would research recipes for vegetarians or pescatarians, they were not so kid-friendly. I don't know about you, but my son was not interested in eggplant and quinoa at 6 years old.

Being a "new" pescatarian mom, I was never comfortable with the "you eat whatever I cook" parenting method. I already felt like I was limiting his selections through diet, within reason. Therefore, I would go above and beyond to create wonderful experiences centered around his meals, ensuring there was no FOMO* present! Additionally, it was important for me to set a good foundation for his future relationship with food. It is an ongoing journey, believe me.

I knew I couldn't be alone in this struggle, so one night after a long day of exhaustion and another day of overthinking the dinner menu, I decided to contribute a solution to this headache.

*FOMO = FEELING OF MISSING OUT

DISCLAIMER

This is a recipe book, not a cookbook, that suggests healthy meals for those with pescatarian diets, with an emphasis on child-friendly selections.

I am not a Chef, and the fact that I am creating a guide for others based on food is a bit ludicrous to me because I do not love to cook. However, I have found a way to make it work, and I believe in spreading love and light.

TABLE OF CONTENTS

LET'S GET STARTED!

1. **Total Time Spent.**

   The purpose is to save time, so I want to ensure you can plan according to your schedule, not just your ingredients.

2. **The Leftover Rating.**

   As a busy mom, leftovers are golden! Sometimes I choose my recipe based on the likelihood of having leftovers, which will save me time the next day. A bonus is if it can be frozen and used as a lifesaver on an upcoming unexpected busy or lazy day.

3. **Fun Substitutions and Sides.**

   Any of these recipes can become a new meal when you mix and match sides and replace the main ingredients with another!

4. **Air Fryer vs Oven vs Stove Top:**

   Either one can work for any recipe. However, it does make a difference which method is used for different recipes.

TUNA "MEAT" BALLS & SPAGHETTI

Hear me out: I know that tuna doesn't sound like it belongs here, but your taste buds will thank me later!

Total Time Spent: 1.5 hours including prep

Leftover Rating: Great for the next few days; however, the kids will devour those tuna balls, with or without the sides. It does not last more than two days in my house!

OVEN over Air-fryer: although both will work, the oven allows the tuna balls to cook more evenly throughout.

Ingredients:

- 2 Cans of canned tuna (2 cans = 10-12 tuna balls)
- 1 onion, chopped (optional)
- 1 green pepper, chopped (optional) Almond Flour
- 1 Egg beat, (per 2 cans) Seasoning of choice spaghetti pasta
- 1 can of Marinara Sauce

Prep:

1. Chop your onions and green peppers.
2. Drain and mix canned tuna in a bowl. Use a fork to break in down into a mush.
3. Add chopped onions and peppers to the mashed tuna, then mix.
4. Mix in desired seasonings (I use garlic powder, Tony Chachere's mixed seasoning, and black pepper)
5. Beat and mix in the egg.
6. Add Almond Flour, $\frac{1}{4}$ cup per 2 cans.
7. Here is where the kids can help. Use a spoon to measure the size of the tuna balls.
   a. Add the mix in your palm to form little balls.
   b. TIP: Use a cupcake pan for the tuna balls instead of a flat baking sheet.
8. Place the tuna balls in the cupcake pan or lay evenly on a baking dish.
9. Drizzle olive oil on top using a spoon to measure the amount disbursed.
10. Heat oven at 400 and bake for 20 minutes on one side.
11. Flip the balls and bake for another 20 minutes.
12. Boil spaghetti noodles in a separate pot.
13. Cook and season the marinara sauce to your preferred taste.

Once Everything is ready, serve accordingly and enjoy!

Fun substitutions:

- Replace tuna with canned salmon
- Replace Almond flour with breadcrumbs or crushed Ritz crackers.
- Replace Spaghetti with any other type of pasta.
- Instead of Tuna Balls, make it a Tuna Patty.

NOLA RED BEANS W/ RICE

This is an easy-peasy cultural favorite! Growing up in New Orleans, red beans and rice are a weekly signature dish served every Monday by most. You can pair it with fried fish or a salad.

Total Time Spent: 2-4 hours, including prep

Leftover Rating: 10 out of 10! You can freeze for months. Place half of the finished pot in a container in the freezer!

OVEN over Air-fryer: Neither, Stove Top!

Prep:

1. Rinse and clean your beans.
   a. Pour them into a large pot and soak in water (30min - 24 hours)
      i. The longer they soak, the softer they get and the shorter the cook time.
   b. Discard any damaged beans

2. Once clean and ready to cook, bring the pot to a boil and fill it with water.
   a. Measured: 10-12 cups of water
   b. Eyeballing method: fill to the screws in the pot

3. Chop your onions, green peppers, and garlic.

4. Add the chopped veggies to the pot of water.

5. Add a stick of butter
   a. I cut my stick into 4 before adding it to the pot

6. Add 4-6 Bay leaves

7. Add the first round of seasoning

8. Stir and bring the mix to a boil

9. Turn the heat down to medium-high

10. Continue to monitor and stir

11. Once the beans soften, use the back of the spoon to mush the beans to the side of the pot and stir

12. Continue monitoring, mushing beans, and stirring until water is dissolved, beans are soft and creamy.
   a. This can take 1-2 hours

13. Once the consistency is right, add another stick of butter if you desire it to be creamier and season to taste. and turn the heat down to low.

14. Steam rice in a separate pot.

To serve: add rice to a boil and pour beans on top. Add hot sauce for extra pleasure!

Ingredients:

- 1 bag of red beans
  Camellia's beans preferred
- 2 sticks of butter
- Bay leaves
- Seasoning of Choice
- 1 Onion, chopped
- 1 green pepper, chopped
- 1 stick of celery, chopped (optional)
- 1 clove of garlic, chopped
  Or be like me and buy the minced garlic :)
- White rice preferred
- BONUS: Hot sauce!

Fun substitutions:

- Fried Fish (we use the fry daddy)
- Fresh Salad
- Potato Salad

COCONUT CURRY SALMON

This healthy recipe was a hit for my picky eater. This is a flavorful twist on salmon. Also, a great way to sneak in bites of ginger and garlic.

Total Time Spent: 2 hours, including prep

Leftover Rating: This meal does not produce a substantial portion for leftovers, giving it a very low leftover rating. If you're lucky, you will have enough left over for 1-2 servings.

OVEN over Air-fryer: Neither, Stove Top!

Ingredients:

- 2-3 salmon fillets
- 2-3 knobs of ginger, minced
- 1 onion, minced
- 1 green pepper, minced
- Olive Oil
- 1 can of coconut milk
- 1 stick of celery, chopped (optional)
- Jamaican curry powder
- Seasoning of choice
- Rice of choice

TIP: Tongs will be most helpful!

Prep:

1. Make your rice: Cook rice according to the package and desired texture
2. Clean the salmon and pat dry
3. Season to your taste
4. Add olive oil to a deep skillet on the stovetop, on medium-high heat
5. Once heated, add salmon, skin-side down
6. Cook on both sides for 5 minutes or until cooked through
7. Once finished, add to a plate and remove skin.
8. Return the skillet to the stovetop. DO NOT RINSE
9. Add a tablespoon of olive oil
10. Sauté garlic, onion, peppers, and ginger
11. Add coconut milk to the skillet and stir.
12. Add the salmon back to the mixture. I like to use a fork to break the salmon into small bites, but you can leave it as a fillet if desired.
13. Reduce heat to medium-low
14. Add your desired amount of curry powder (it should change colors to a more yellow-orange color)
15. Cover and let it cook down for 2-4 minutes.
16. Taste and add any seasoning to desired taste.

Serving: Spoon rice in a bowl, add coconut curry salmon and mixture over rice for a delectable, healthy dinner!!

VEGGIE LASAGNA

This classic needs no introduction; however, it is my favorite way to sneak in veggies like zucchini and squash into my picky eater's diet.

Total Time Spent: 2 hours, including prep

Leftover Rating: 10 out of 10! This recipe stores
very well. Pro Tip: Make 2 pans, the second pan is for leftovers only. Cut the lasagna into single portions and wrap individually before freezing. This allows single servings rather than defrosting all at once.

OVEN over Air-fryer: Keep it old school, Oven!

Tip: I like using disposable pans for this recipe to save dishes, and the pans offer more depth and space. For more layers!

Ingredients:

- Butter   (If making 2 pans, double it!)
- 1 egg
- 1 bell pepper, chopped 1
- garlic, chopped
- 1 yellow onion, chopped
- 1 medium zucchini, chopped
- 1 medium yellow squash, chopped
- 1 bag of spinach
- 2 cans of Mariana sauce
- Large ricotta cheese
- 1 bag of shredded Mexican-mix cheese,
- 1 bag of Parmesan cheese
- 1 bag of mozzarella cheese
- 3 boxes of no-boil lasagna noodles
- Seasoning of choice

Prep:

1. Preheat oven to 400 degrees.
2. Wash and clean your disposable pans and let them dry as we follow the next steps.
3. Chop everything and have it ready to go before starting the recipe.
4. In a mixing bowl, add chopped zucchini and squash and season to taste. Set to the side.
5. In a large pot (5-8 quarts, the same size pot you made the red beans in) add olive oil to create your filling.
6. Once heated, add chopped onions, peppers, and garlic to the pot and cook down.
7. Add zucchini and squash to the mix and cook down until soft.
8. Turn the heat down to medium and add one can of marinara sauce to the veggies.
9. Mix and season to taste (don't overdo it because the veggies were pre-seasoned).
10. Once cooked to taste, remove from the heat. Mix in the spinach. This is your filling!
11. In a separate bowl, beat the egg.
12. Add the ricotta cheese and the egg to a separate bowl, mix, and set aside.
13. Use butter to lightly grease your clean and DRY disposable pan or dish.
14. Add 1-2 tablespoons of the Mariana sauce to the bottom and spread across the entire bottom of the pan.
15. Layer the lasagna noodles along the bottom of the pan. (Sometimes you have to break one to fill the sides.)
16. Add ricotta cheese on top of the "filling" (use half)
17. Add "your filling" over the first layer of lasagna noodles (use half)
18. Evenly sprinkle mozzarella cheese, parmesan cheese, and Mexican cheese mix on top of the ricotta.
19. Add another layer of lasagna noodles and repeat the steps above, using the remaining half of ricotta and "filling".
20. Add a third layer of lasagna noodles. (This is the top)
21. Lightly spread any extra sauce on the top layer of noodles (no veggies)
22. Evenly spread the remaining mozzarella cheese, parmesan cheese, and Mexican cheese mix on top.
23. Cover with foil and bake for 30 minutes.
    a. If the mixture is watery, poke small holes in the corner of the pan and drain. Then return to the oven for another 10-15 minutes
24. Let it sit to cool before serving.
25. Taste even better the next day!

PESTO PASTA W/ SHRIMP

Pesto on anything please! This easy recipe is my elevated version of the traditional spaghetti meal!

Total Time Spent: 40 minutes including prep

Leftover Rating: Great for the next day or 2!

OVEN over Air-fryer: Stove top!

Ingredients:

- 1 box of bowtie pasta
- 1-2 lbs. of shrimp (fresh is always better than frozen)
- 1 can of pesto sauce
- ½ onion, minced
- 1 green pepper, minced
- 1 garlic, minced
- Olive Oil

Prep:

1. Peel, devein, and wash the shrimp.
2. Season the shrimp to taste in a bowl and set aside.
3. Chop your onions, green peppers, and garlic, and set them aside.
4. Boil and drain the pasta. Set to the side
5. In Skillett, melt a tbsp of butter per pound of shrimp.
6. Once butter is melted, add onions, green peppers, and garlic.
7. Sautee and cook the veggies down.
8. Once veggies are browning, add shrimp to the skillet
9. Sautee and mix the shrimp with the veggies (add more butter if necessary)
10. Once the shrimp are pink and cooked, remove the skillet from the heat.
11. Prepare the sauce: In a separate pan/saucer, add the pesto sauce
12. Cook down to desired consistency.
    a. I usually don't add ingredients to pesto sauce
    b. However, if using Marinara or Alfredo sauce, I do add additional seasoning
13. Add cooked shrimp and veggies to the pesto sauce and mix, all of it!
14. Cook on medium for 3-4 minutes
15. Add pasta to bowl, top with shrimp pesto mix, and enjoy!

Fun substitutions:

- Replace Shrimp with Baked Salmon.
- Replace Bowtie pasta with any other type of pasta.
- Replace pesto sauce with any pasta sauce.
- You don't have to mix the shrimp in the sauce.
- Add any veggies to the mix that your picky eater may enjoy.

WALNUT TACOS WITH HOME-MADE PICO

**A meat lover would never know the difference!
These tacos are a hit and fun to make.**

Total Time Spent: 1.5 hours including prep

Leftover Rating: This question is subjective to your household and to the quantity you make!

OVEN over Air-fryer: Stove top!

Ingredients:

- 1 can of chickpeas (optional)
- 1 onion, chopped (optional)
- 1 -2 chopped bell peppers
- 2 tomatoes, chopped
- one cucumber
- Black Pepper
- Himalayan Salt
- Olive Oil - for Pico and Walnuts
- Vegetable oil - for taco shells
- Tortillas or premade taco shells
- One bag of crushed Walnuts
- Taco sauce
- Don't forget the sour cream!

Prep:

1. Enhanced Pico
    a. Wash chickpeas and add to a large container
    b. Chop up tomatoes and add to the bowl with the chickpeas
    c. Chop1-2 bell peppers of choice and mix
    d. Chop one onion and add to the mix
    e. Chop one cucumber and add to the mix
    f. Mix all veggies
    g. Season with olive oil, Himalayan salt, and black pepper
    h. cover, shake, to mix (best cold)

2. Walnuts - Stove Top!
    a. Add 1-2 tablespoons of water to a skillet and heat it.
    b. Add chopped walnuts to the pan, stir frequently, and cook down until soft.
    c. Add chopped peppers, onions, and garlic.
    d. Cook and mix for 3-5 minutes or until veggies are soft.
    e. Add desired seasoning and cook down.
    f. Add taco sauce, mix and stir.
    g. Remove from heat, and mix.
    h. Add Mexican shredded cheese to the mixture.

3. Hard Taco Shells - Stove Top! I learned this in Palm Springs :)
    a. Heat vegetable oil in a small skillet.
    b. While the oil heats, set up a drain station and grab a fork (I'll explain later). Drain plate: Place paper plates on a plate near the fire.
    c. Once oil is fully heated, add one tortilla to the oil, lay flat.
    d. Once it starts to harden. use a fork to fold one side of the tortilla over "like a taco."
    e. Use a fork to fold, and let fry hard or until golden.
    f. Use a fork to drain and remove for oil from the plate.
    g. Hang upside down for draining.
    h. Repeat for the desired number of hard shells.
    i. You can definitely use boxed taco shells too! Try the Dorito Shells, yum!

Fun substitutions:

- Replace Walnuts with Jackfruit.
- Try with Dorito taco shells!
- Try with hard tacos or soft tacos.

Add toppings and make your tacos!

SALMON ENCHILADAS

We eat a lot of salmon, so we are always trying to find creative ways to serve it.
Don't forget the sour cream and sides!

Total Time Spent: 2 hours, including prep

Leftover Rating: Another 10 out of 10, provided they last more than one day, lol. My son cannot stop eating them. They may last 2 days in our house.

OVEN over Air-fryer: Definitely the Oven!

Prep:

1. Preheat oven to 400
2. Wash and dry the pan for enchiladas (use a separate dish for the salmon)
3. Chop the onions and green peppers
4. Clean salmon (you can either remove the skin here or after baking)
5. Grease the salmon pan with butter.
6. Add salmon to the pan and season to taste.
7. Add chopped onions and peppers to the salmon.
8. Cut slices of butter to layer the salmon and veggies
9. Bake for 20 minutes or until cooked all the way through.
10. As salmon bakes, work on your sides.
11. Once the salmon is finished, remove the pan from the oven, let it cool.
12. In the same dish, remove skin if you haven't already.
13. Add 1-2 cans of enchilada sauce to the salmon mixture.
14. Stir everything and mush the salmon together.
15. Add cheese, raw spinach, and any other desired filling.
16. Make sure to use enough enchilada sauce so that the mixture is moist
17. Grease the enchilada disposable tin pan with butter.
18. I highly suggest you prep your station before starting the process.
19. BONUS: Warm the tortillas in the microwave for 10-13 seconds one by one before filling.
20. Process to make the enchiladas:
    a. Warm tortilla
    b. Add filling to the desired thickness
    c. Roll tortilla in pan
    d. push to the side to make room for the next enchilada
21. Repeat the process until the pan is full
22. Pour the final can of enchilada sauce on top of the rolled enchiladas
23. Add cheese
24. Bake for 20 minutes
25. Top with sour cream and cilantro

Ingredients:

- 1 large salmon (the entire salmon)
- 1 onion, chopped (optional)
- 1 green pepper, chopped (optional)
- 3-4 cans of enchilada sauce
- 10-12 tortillas/ 2 bags (I like the smaller ones)
- 2 bags of Mexican shredded cheese
- ½ stick of butter
- Seasoning of choice
- Sour cream
- Cilantro
- Black olives (Optional)
- Veggies (Optional)

TIP: Use disposable tin pans!

Serve with one of these SIDES:

- Rice & Beans
- Yellow Rice
- Sweet Plantains
- Salad of Choice
- Sauteed Spinach
- Sour Cream

BAKED SALMON & GRITS

Every southern home has grits! Here is a twist on having breakfast for dinner. Add a succulent salmon filet, and let the grits soak up the flavor!

Total Time Spent: 45 minutes, including prep

Leftover Rating: Not a good leftover rating. This is one serving per person.

OVEN over Air-fryer: Salmon in the air fryer, grits on the stove top!

Ingredients:

- Grits
- 1 onion, chopped (optional)
- 1 green pepper, chopped (optional)
- 2 sticks of butter
- 1 Salmon Fillet per person
- Seasoning of choice
- Salt and Pepper for this one!
- Olive Oil

Follow the recipe for grits:

a. My TIP is to add half a stick of butter per 2 servings to make grits creamy
b. Also, add pepper

Salmon Prep:

1. Chop the onions and green peppers
2. Clean and Season salmon fillets
3. Add chopped onions and peppers to the top salmon
4. Drizzle olive oil
5. Bake in Air Fryer at 325 for 25 minutes

Plating it

- Add grits to the center of the plate.
- Place the Salmon and veggies on top of the grits.

Fun substitutions:

- Replace salmon with shrimp
- Replace salmon with fried whiting
- Replace grits with waffles or pancakes

Add-ons:

- Add breakfast potatoes
- Add breakfast eggs

NOLA SHRIMP PO-BOYS

Another New Orleans classic that is easy to make at home, whether you have all of the ingredients or not!

Total Time Spent: 1 hour, including prep

Leftover Rating: It does not typically last long. This meal is consumed on one night.

OVEN over Air-fryer: Stove Top!

Prep:

1. Clean, peel, and devein shrimp

2. Add vegetable oil in a large frying pan and let it get hot (frying level)
   a. want it to be at a bowl before adding shrimp
   b. Test with a small piece of onion

3. As the oil heats up, beat the eggs in a bowl

4. Put the fish fry in a large Ziploc bag for easy mixing

5. Drain plate: Place paper plates on a plate near the fryer

6. Once the oil is ready to fry, follow the following process
   a. Mix 5-6 shrimp in egg batter
   b. Once covered evenly, mix those same shrimps in the fish fry Ziplock
   c. Once covered in batter
   d. Move shrimp to the fryer
   e. They should start browning in 2-3 minutes or until golden in color
   f. Transfer from the oil to the drain plate

7. Repeat this process with all shrimp

8. Warm bread

9. Add condiments

10. Add shrimp

11. Drizzle with hot sauce and ketchup

Ingredients:

- 2 pounds of cleaned, peeled, and deveined shrimp
- 2 eggs beaten
- Tony Chachere's Cajun Fish Fry
- Vegetable Oil
- Bread of Choice
  o The authentic bread is French Bread
  o I like potato rolls instead ;)
- Preferred sandwich toppings
  o mayo
  o ketchup
  o hot sauce (we like the Crystals and Louisiana brands)
  o lettuce or spinach
  o tomatoes
  o dill pickles
  o cheese (optional)

Enjoy!

Fun substitution:
- Bread of Choice

AFUW'S EXTRA SPECIAL SAUCE

Afuw's palate is maturing, and he is 1000% interested in what he eats.
He likes flavors, sauces, and dips! Check out this BONUS recipe from Afuw that
can add an extra zest to your pescatarian options.

Mix the following ingredients together in a bowl.
There aren't any specific measurements, eyeball it.

1. Himalayan pink salt
2. Tony Chachere's Cajun Seasoning
3. Garlic Powder
4. Lemon Juice (better if freshly squeezed)
5. Cayenne Pepper
6. Louisiana brand hot sauce
7. Mayonnaise
8. Ketchup

FUN SIDES THAT GO WITH EVERYTHING!

- Barbeque Chickpeas
- Stuffed Bell Peppers
- Garlic Mashed Potatoes
- Mac n Cheese
- Broccoli Casserole
- Sweet Carrots
- Lemon herb Asparagus
- Grilled Pineapples
- Seasoned Brown Rice
- Couscous
- Sauteed Spinach

A SOLUTION
FOR
BUSY MOMS

A SOLUTION
FOR
BUSY MOMS

AUNTEA MUHAMMAD & AFUW MUHAMMAD JR

www.ingramcontent.com/pod-product-compliance
Lightning Source LLC
Chambersburg PA
CBHW051254120626
46547CB00014B/1938